W9-ATJ-092

WORDS OF WISDOM
FOR PARENTS

WORDS OF WISDOM FOR PARENTS

Time-tested thoughts on how to raise kids

edited by
Charles E. Schaefer, Ph.D.

JASON ARONSON INC.
Northvale, New Jersey
London

Production Editor: Elaine Lindenblatt
Interior Book Design: Nancy J. D'Arrigo

This book was printed and bound by Book-mart Press of North Bergen, New Jersey.

Library of Congress Cataloging-in-Publication Data

Words of wisdom for parents : time-tested thoughts on how to raise
    kids / edited by Charles E. Schaefer.
        p.   cm.
    Includes bibliographical references and index.
    ISBN 1-56821-797-8 (alk. paper)
    1. Child rearing—Quotations, maxims, etc.   2. Parenting—
Quotations, maxims, etc.   I. Schaefer, Charles E.
PN6084.C48W67   1996
649'1—dc20   95-52073

Manufactured in the United States of America. Jason Aronson Inc. offers books and cassettes. For information and catalog write to Jason Aronson Inc., 230 Livingston Street, Northvale, New Jersey 07647.

He is a benefactor of mankind who contracts the great rules of life into short sentences that may be easily impressed on the memory, and so recur habitually to mind.

—Samuel Johnson

Child Therapy Series

A series of books edited by
CHARLES SCHAEFER

Therapeutic Use of Child's Play
Charles Schaefer, ed.

Clinical Handbook of Sleep Disorders in Children
Charles Schaefer, ed.

Clinical Handbook of Anxiety Disorders
in Children and Adolescents
*Andrew R. Eisen, Christopher A. Kearney,
and Charles Schaefer, eds.*

Practitioner's Guide to Treating Fear and
Anxiety in Children and Adolescents:
A Cognitive-Behavioral Approach
Andrew R. Eisen and Christopher A. Kearney

Words of Wisdom for Parents: Time-Tested
Thoughts on How to Raise Kids
Charles Schaefer, ed.

The Playing Cure: Individualized Play Therapy
for Specific Childhood Problems
*Heidi Kaduson, Donna Cangelosi,
and Charles Schaefer, eds.*

Table of Contents

Introduction

My idea of a really good book is one in which great people talk to us and give us their most precious thoughts. This was my goal in compiling this quotation book.

The pressures and problems faced by parents and children today have never been greater. Unfortunately, children do not come with instruction manuals and parents receive little or no preparation for parenthood from our educational system. Support from extended family is also not readily available in our mobile society. Parents today know they need advice and are turning more and more to books and support groups to obtain it.

In this era of "how to," with specialized advice books on every topic from how to improve your backswing to how to make a will, it occurred to me that no book exists that brings together the best advice, over centuries, centering on how to raise children.

What better advice could parents obtain than the common sense about parenting that has been passed down from those who have raised their own kids? In 1748, Lord Chesterfield wrote in a letter to his son, "Common sense (which, in truth, is very uncommon) is the best sense I know of. Abide by it, it will counsel you best." Similarly, Lord Bramwell said, "What are maxims but the expression of that which good sense has made a rule." Until now, the wisdom of the ages has been widely scattered and unavailable to parents.

Advice that is not remembered is of no use to anyone. Accordingly, this book contains short, well-worded quotes on parenting that are easily remembered. A book such as this, which contains the most insights in the fewest words, seems tailor-made for today's busy parent.

The quotes in this book are obtained from a thorough review of the literature, both modern and ancient. Three criteria were used to select the best quotations: degree of wisdom, conciseness, and eloquence of expression. The quotations are grouped within twenty-two broadly defined subject categories; for example, love, discipline, responsibility, and family life. Within these categories, the quotes are listed alphabetically by author.

The book is meant to be a handy and regular companion to parents as they go through the stages of childrearing—infancy through adolescence. Hopefully, parents will frequently refer to this treasury of advice as they seek to refine and expand their parenting practices.

Most likely, the parents who will prize this volume the most are those who are themselves wise, for as Ralph Waldo Emerson once observed, "The profoundest thought or passion sleeps as in a mine, until an equal mind and heart finds it." Of course, we are not apt to agree with all the advice contained in this book, but the maxims give us something to react to so as to clarify our own beliefs.

Some of the quotations come from secondary sources, and have probably been polished with repeated use; read them more for the wisdom they contain than for the scholarly certainty about the original phrasing.

A book of quotations can never be finished. I would welcome your comments for additional quotations.

Charles E. Schaefer, Ph.D.
139 Temple Avenue
Hackensack, NJ 07601

1

LOVING
YOUR CHILD

Parents love their children more
than children love their parents.

—Anonymous

❧

Another day gone and not once did
I say "I love you." Dear Lord, forgive
me.

—Anonymous

❧

Our love for our children must not
hinge on response.

—Anonymous

❧

No one loves the man whom
he fears.

—Aristotle

3

There is no friendship, no love like that of the parent for the child.

—Henry Ward Beecher

We never know the love of our parents until we become parents.

—Henry Ward Beecher

One touch is worth ten thousand words.

—Harold Bloomfield
Melba Cosgrove
and Pete McWilliams

Those parents are wise that can fit their nurture according to their nature.

—Anne Bradstreet

It's good for a child to be in the company of people who are crazy about him for a substantial number of hours every day. I'm sure of that. But it is also good to be with people who are not crazy about him. He needs both kinds of experience. He needs some mothers, some fathers, some day care, even some coolness towards him. . . . All of these needs must be met.

—*Urie Bronfenbrenner*

If you love someone, tell him now.

—*Leo Buscaglia*

You have to love your children unselfishly. That's hard. But it's the only way.

—*Barbara Bush*

The first fact we must understand
in order to have a well-disciplined
child is that making a child feel loved
is the first and most important part of
good discipline.

—*Dr. Ross Campbell*

And here's the whole challenge of
being a parent. Even though your kids
will consistently do the exact opposite
of what you tell them to do, you have
to keep loving them just as much.

—*Bill Cosby*

Say "I love you" to those you love.
The eternal silence is long enough to
be silent in, and that awaits us all.

—*George Eliot*

6

There are so many disciplines in being a parent besides the obvious ones like getting up in the night and putting up with the noise during the day. And almost the hardest of all is learning to be a well of affection, and not a fountain, to show them we love them, not when we feel like it, but when they do.

—*Nan Fairbrother*

If you can't hold them in your arms, please hold them in your heart.

—*Lorraine Hall*

The supreme happiness of life is the conviction of being loved for yourself, or, more correctly, being loved in spite of yourself.

—*Victor Hugo*

Children need love, especially
when they do not deserve it.
—Harold Hulbert

To be told one is loved is not
enough. We must feel loved.
—Marcia Jacober

Parenting at its best comes as
naturally as laughter. It's automatic,
involuntary, unconditional love.
—Sally James

Love doesn't sit there like a stone,
it has to be made, like bread;
remade all the time, made new.
—Ursula K. Le Guin

8

To love is to place our happiness in the happiness of another.

—Leibnitz

❧

To cease to be loved is for the child practically synonymous with ceasing to live.

—Dr. Karl A. Menninger

❧

If we suddenly discovered that we had only five minutes left to say all we wanted to say, every telephone booth would be occupied by people trying to call up other people to tell them that they loved them.

—Christopher Morley

❧

If you judge people, you have no time to love them.

—Mother Teresa

There is one sure way to remind
children of their connection to life
and other human beings and that
they are important and valuable—
it's called a hug.

—*Lauren Munger*

❧

Every child deserves to believe
that she or he is truly a wonder.

—*Lauren Murphy Payne*

❧

Sometimes the poorest man leaves
his children the richest inheritances.

—*Ruth E. Renkel*

Nothing can replace the influence of
unconditional love in the life of a
child.

—*Fred Rogers*

∽◎

You can't really love someone else
unless you really love yourself first.

—*Fred Rogers*

∽◎

I think I like myself because I am
loved so much.

—*Rory, age 10*

∽◎

Give a little love to a child and
you'll get a great deal back.

—*John Ruskin*

Oh, how little do children know
what parents sometimes endure
for their sake!

—*Mary Martha Sherwood*

❧

Perhaps a child who is fussed
over gets a feeling of destiny; he
thinks he's in the world for
something important and it
gives him drive and confidence.

—*Dr. Benjamin Spock*

❧

Love is an art of endless
forgiveness, a tender look
which becomes a habit.

—*Peter Ustinov*

12

Parents must get across the idea that, I love you always, but sometimes I do not love your behavior.

—*Amy Vanderbilt*

PRAISE/
ENCOURAGEMENT

If you keep telling your son something's wrong with him, sooner or later he'll believe it. Follow every "that's wrong" by saying what's right.

—*John E. Anderson*

❧

I praise loudly; I blame softly.

—*Catherine II of Russia*

❧

Dads, give us more compliments and fewer putdowns.

—*Chris, age 12*

Praise children for important things,
even if you have to stretch them a bit.
Praise them a lot. They live on
it like bread and butter, and they
need it more than bread and butter.

–Lavina Fugal,
on being chosen Mother of the Year, 1955

It is more difficult to praise rightly
than to blame.

–*Thomas Fuller*

We live by encouragement and die
without it—slowly, sadly, and angrily.

–*Celeste Holm*

P raise the young and they will blossom.

—Irish Proverb

❧

A child is fed with milk and praise.

—Mary Lamb

❧

C old words freeze people, and hot words scorch them, and bitter words make them bitter, and wrathful words make them wrathful. Kind words also provide their own image on men's souls; and a beautiful image it is. They soothe, and quiet, and comfort the hearer.

—Blaise Pascal

See everything, overlook a lot, correct a little.

—*Pope John XXIII*

⊘⁄⊘

Encourage one another and build one another up.

—*St. Paul's Epistle*
Thessalonians 5:11

⊘⁄⊘

I have yet to find the man—however exalted his station—who did not do better work and put forth greater effort under a spirit of approval than under a spirit of criticism.

—*Charles Schwab*

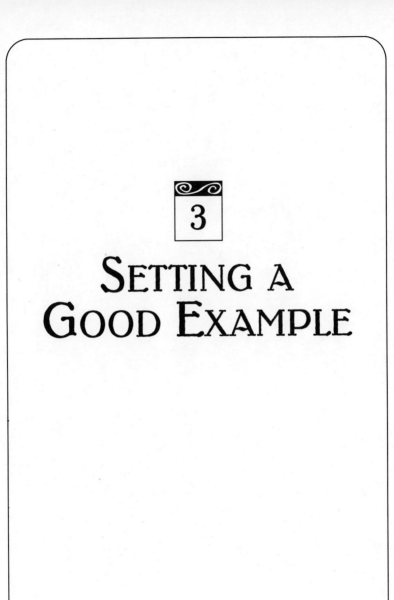

3

SETTING A GOOD EXAMPLE

Children have never been
very good at listening to their
elders, but they have never failed
to imitate them.

—*James Baldwin*

❧

Whenever a parent gives his
children good instruction and sets
them at the same time a bad
example, he may be considered
as bringing them food in one
hand and poison in the other.

—*Balguy*

❧

To bring up a child in the way he
should go, travel that way yourself
once in a while.

—*Josh Billings*

Children naturally want to be like
their parents, and to do what they do.
— *William Cobbett*

❧

I talk and talk and talk, and I
haven't taught people in fifty years
what my father taught me by
example in one week.
— *Mario Cuomo*

❧

A good example is like a bell that
calls many to church.
— *Danish Proverb*

The only good advice is good example. You don't tell them a whole lot of anything. You show them by doing. You teach values by making choices in their presence. They see what you do and they make judgments on it.

—Ossie Davis

Example is always the best teacher—and what we do always overwhelms and overshadows and outteaches what we say.

—Linda and Richard Eyre

You can preach a better sermon with your life than with your lips.

—Oliver Goldsmith

The reason parents no longer
lead their children in the right
direction is that parents aren't
going that way themselves.

—Ken Hubbard

Children have more need of
models than of critics.

—Joubert

If there is anything that we wish to
change in the child, we should first
examine it and see whether it is not
something that could be better
changed in ourselves.

—Carl Jung

Children learn as much from observing adults, and then imitating and modeling our behavior, as they do from actual instruction. This means that parents must constantly demonstrate by their own actions and behavior what they are telling their children to do. The child gets two confusing messages when a parent tells him which is the right fork to use, and then proceeds to use the wrong one. So does the child who listens to parents bicker and fuss, yet is told to be nice to his brothers and sisters.

—Dr. Michael Lewis

But I think parents aren't teachers anymore. Parents—or a whole lot of us, at least—lead by mouth instead of by example.

—Robert R. McCammon

What's done to children, they will do to society.

−*Dr. Karl A. Menninger*

A good example is the best sermon.

−*Proverb*

Thou canst not rebuke in children what they see practiced in thee. Till reason be ripe, examples direct more than precepts. Such as is thy behavior before thy children's faces, such is theirs behind thy back.

−*Quarles*

Example is not the main thing in influencing others; it is the only thing.

−*Albert Schweitzer*

N o legacy is so rich as honesty.
—*William Shakespeare*

W hatever you would have your children become, strive to exhibit in your own lives and conversation.
—*Mrs. Sigourney*

DISCIPLINE

The tongue is the deadliest of all blunt instruments.

—Anonymous

It's important to let people know what you stand for. It's equally important that they know what you won't stand for.

—B. Bader

There was a time when we expected nothing of children but obedience, as opposed to the present, when we expect everything of them but obedience.

—Anotole Broyard

33

Children can stand vast amounts of sternness. They rather expect to be wrong, and are quite used to being punished. It is injustice, inequity, and inconsistency that kill them.

—*Robert F. Capon*

❧

The worst ruler is one who cannot rule himself.

—*Cato*

❧

Let the punishment match the offense.

—*Cicero*

❧

What has one who is not able to govern himself to do with governing others.

—*Confucius*

34

If a family wants to get through the day with a minimum of noise and open wounds, the parents have to impose order on the domestic scene.

—*Bill Cosby*

Unrestricted freedom has made tyrants of children and slaves of parents.

—*Rudolf Dreikurs*

Without order, there can be no freedom.

—*Rudolf Dreikurs*

The thing that impresses me most about America is the way parents obey their children.

—*Duke of Windsor*

Of nineteen out of twenty things
in children, take no special notice;
but if as to the twentieth, you give
a direction or command, see that
you are obeyed.

—*Tryon Edwards*

The certainty of punishment,
even more than the severity, is
the prevention of crime.

—*Tryon Edwards*

Our chief want in life is someone
who will make us do what we can.

—*Ralph Waldo Emerson*

If you command wisely, you'll be
obeyed cheerfully.

—*Thomas Fuller*

To punish and not prevent is to labor
at the pump and leave open the leak.
                    —Thomas Fuller

❧

Discipline comes from the same
root as disciple, which means "pupil"
or "learner." It suggests that our func-
tion as parents is to guide or teach
rather than judge.

                    —Louise Hart

❧

Discipline is guidance, not punishment.
You are teaching what is appropriate
behavior and what is inappropriate.
                    —Dot Hattich

❧

An infallible way to make your
child miserable is to satisfy all his
demands.

                    —Henry Home (Lord Kames)

Patience has its limits. Take it too far, and it's cowardice.

—*George Jackson*

The art of being wise is the art of knowing what to overlook.

—*William James*

Parents fail a child if they allow her to do anything that makes them dislike her as well as her action.

—*Penelope Leach*

Ask your child what he wants for dinner only if he's buying.

—*Fran Lebowitz*

A torn jacket is soon mended,
but hard words bruise the heart
of a child.

—*Henry Wadsworth Longfellow*

❧

He that would govern others, first
should be the master of himself.

—*Philip Massinger*

❧

Where does discipline end? Where
does cruelty begin? Somewhere
between these, thousands of children
inhabit a voiceless hell.

—*François Mauriac*

❧

The word *no* carries a lot more
meaning when spoken by a parent
who also knows how to say *yes.*

—*Joyce Maynard*

Bringing up children and training
horses aren't so terribly different.
With horses it's no good letting
them boss you around in the stable
and expect them to be saints outside.
Same with children. It's no good
letting them come home from school
and rampage around the house and
then express surprise that their school
report says they're too boisterous.
On the whole, animals are easier,
because they don't answer back.

—Princess Anne of England

The surest way to make it hard for
children is to make it easy for them.

—Eleanor Roosevelt

Frequent punishments are always a
sign of weakness or laziness on the
part of the government.

—Jean-Jacques Rousseau

Your child must not get what he
wants, but what he needs.

—Jean-Jacques Rousseau

Obedience is in a way the mother
of all virtues.

—St. Augustine

Say "Yes!" to your children as
often as you can.

—Anne W. Schaefer

Your sons weren't made to like you.
That's what grandchildren are for.

—Jane Smiley

41

If all parents today were as strict as I was, we wouldn't have so many brats and little vandals.

—*Dr. Benjamin Spock's mother*

❧

I have thought about it a great deal, and the more I think, the more certain I am that obedience is the gateway through which knowledge, yes, and love, too, enter the mind of the child.

—*Annie Sullivan*

❧

Parent(s), if you are a nonsmoking, nondrinking, churchgoing, consistent, family-oriented, loving disciplinarian, the odds are overwhelmingly in your favor that you will raise a positive drug-free child.

—*Dr. Forest Tennent*

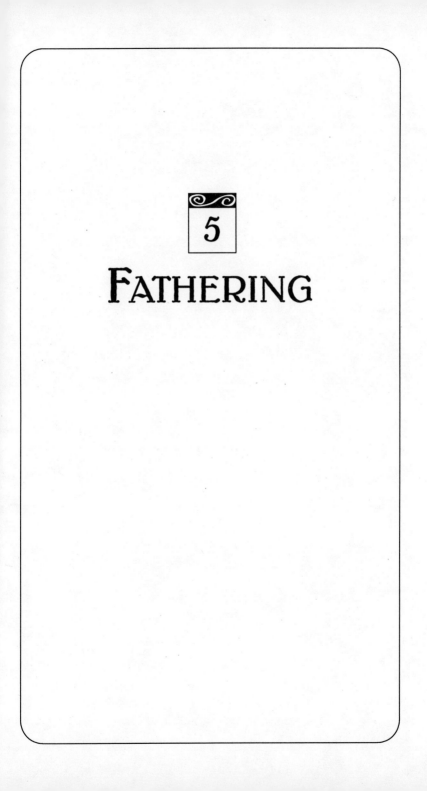

5

FATHERING

Father! Father! Where are you going?
Oh do not walk so fast. Speak,
father, speak to your little boy
or else I shall be lost.

—*William Blake*

❧❧

To become a father is not hard.
To be a father is, however.

—*Wilhelm Busch*

❧❧

The father is the initiating priest
through whom the young being
passes into the larger world.

—*Joseph Campbell*

❧❧

A father who takes care of his child
physically and emotionally is not a
mothering father, but a father pure
and simple—he gives reality to a
word that until now has remained
empty of meaning.

—*Guy Corneau*

45

The nurturing father is not the product of recent times, but is a man whose feelings of self-esteem are as invested in his children and his ability to be a loving parent as in his work and career.

–Louise Genevie and Eva Margolies

❧

My father was often angry when I was most like him.

–Lillian Hellman

❧

One father is more than a hundred schoolmasters.

–George Herbert

❧

When one has not had a good father, one must create one!

–Friedrich Nietzsche

46

Most times, after my mother made dinner, my father would put the apron on and do the dishes, and that was never beneath him. . . . It didn't even occur to him that it might make him look wimpy or henpecked. I definitely picked up that attitude from my dad. And the way I've used it in my own life is by treating women, men, and children with respect.

—Robert Pastorelli

The guys who fear becoming fathers don't understand that fathering is not something perfect men do, but something that perfects the man. The end product of child raising is not the child but the parent.

—Dr. Frank Pittman

The words a father speaks to his children in the privacy of the home are not overheard at the time, but, as in whispering galleries, they will be clearly heard at the end by posterity.

—*Conrad Richter*

The place of the father in the modern suburban family is a very small one, particularly if he plays golf.

—*Bertrand Russell*

The fundamental defect of fathers is that they want their children to be a credit to them.

—*Bertrand Russell*

48

My father had faith in me and loved me. Maybe you don't exactly learn from that, but it allows you to take on the world. I grew up knowing I was accepted and loved, and that made an incredible difference.

—*Dr. Bernie Siegel*

Children know that they need a father figure and will create one out of whatever materials are at hand.

—*Dr. Benjamin Spock*

It's clear that most American children suffer too much mother and too little father.

—*Gloria Steinem*

The father who subordinates his son's interests to his own convenience is a fool; he himself loses, and the situation remains unimproved.

—*Titus Maccius Plutus*

❧

If men do not keep on speaking terms with children, they cease to be men, and become merely machines for eating and for earning money.

—*John Updike*

❧

It's a wonderful feeling when your father becomes not a god, but a man to you—when he comes down from the mountain and you see he's this man with weaknesses. And you love him as this whole being, not as a figurehead.

—*Robin Williams*

6

MOTHERING

6

MOTHERING

The mother's heart is the child's schoolroom.

—*Henry Ward Beecher*

❦

Good mothering . . . imposes just enough frustration to help the ego develop, but no more.

—*Gertrude and Rubin Blanck*

❦

It is not until you become a mother that your judgment slowly turns to compassion and understanding.

—*Erma Bombeck*

❦

Children find comfort in flaws, ignorance, and insecurities similar to their own. I love my mother for letting me see hers.

—*Erma Bombeck*

53

We humans would never know who we were without a mirror to look at in the beginning. That mirror needs to reflect ourselves as the person we really are at any given time. The original mirror is almost always the mothering person who raises us, especially in the first three years of life.

—*John Bradshaw*

We are raised to believe that mother love is different from other kinds of love. It is not open to error, doubt, or to the ambivalence of ordinary affections. This is an illusion. Mothers may love children, but they some-times do not like them. The same woman who may be willing to put her body between her child and a runaway truck will often resent the day-by-day sacrifice the child unknowingly demands of her time, sexuality, and self-development.

—*Nancy Friday*

Moms, take time to play checkers.

—George, age 6

The commonest fallacy among women is that simply having children makes one a mother—which is as absurd as believing that having a piano makes one a musician.

—Sydney J. Harris

Being a mother, as far as I can tell, is a constantly evolving process of adapting to the needs of your child while also changing and growing as a person in your own right.

—Deborah Insel

A father may turn his back on his child; brothers and sisters may become inveterate enemies; husbands may desert their wives and wives their husbands. But a mother's love endures through all; in good repute, in bad repute, in the face of the world's condemnation, a mother still loves on, and still hopes that her child may turn from his evil ways, and repent; still she remembers the infant smiles that once filled her bosom with rapture, the merry laugh, the joyful shout of his childhood, the opening promise of his youth; and she can never be brought to think him all unworthy.

—Washington Irving

In a child's lunch box, a mother's thought.

—*Japanese Proverb*

❧

Babies do not have a fixed quota of love to give, so having more than one person who is "special" to him does not deprive a baby's mother of anything.

—*Penelope Leach*

❧

By and large, mothers and housewives are the only workers who do not have regular time off.

—*Anne Morrow Lindbergh*

❧

Every beetle is a gazelle in the eyes of its mother.

—*Moorish Proverb*

No matter how old a mother is, she
watches her middle-aged children
for signs of improvement.

—Florida Scott-Maxwell

◎◎

An ounce of mother is worth a
pound of clergy.

—Spanish Proverb

7

FAMILY LIFE

A family that plays together, stays together.

—Anonymous

❧

F amily jokes . . . are the bond that keeps most families alive.

—Stella Benson

❧

W hen you look at your life, the greatest happinesses are family happinesses.

—Dr. Joyce Brothers

❧

Y ou must teach your children that the ground beneath their feet is the ashes of their grandfathers.

—Chief Seattle

Nobody's family can hang out the sign, "Nothing the matter here."

—Chinese Proverb

❧

There is no doubt that it is around the family and the home that all the greatest virtues, the most dominating virtues of human society are created, strengthened, and maintained.

—Winston Churchill

❧

What families have in common the world around is that they are the place where people learn who they are and how to be that way.

—Jean Illsley Clarke

[F amily] bonds are formed less by moments of celebration and of crisis than by quiet, undramatic accretion of minutiae—the remark on the way out the door, the chore undone, the unexpected smile.

—*George Howe Colt*

⊘∕⊘

Tradition is to human beings what instinct is to animals.

—*Erik Erikson*

⊘∕⊘

Grown-ups are no fun.
They never have time to
    do things with you . . .
If I could change grown-ups
I would make them do nothing
    but play with you.
But everyone knows that
    you can't do that.

—*A Fifth Grader*

We don't have to achieve to be accepted by our families. We just have to be. Our membership is not based on credentials but on birth.

—*Ellen Goodman*

❧

We think that the ancestors are behind us, but they also go before us—a vanguard, a spirit wave, pulling us along.

—*Joan Halifax*

❧

We are born into a family and, at the last, we rejoin its full extension when gathered to the ancestors. Family grave, family altar, family trust, family secrets, family pride.

—*James Hillman*

Traditions, customs, habits, routines
are all the arrangements which
make everyday life self-starting
and self-regulating.

—Eric Hoffer

Woman knows what Man has too
long forgotten, that the ultimate
economic and spiritual unit of any
civilization is still the family.

—Clare Boothe Luce

The car trip can draw the family
together, as it was in the days before
television when parents and children
actually talked to each other.

—Andrew H. Malcolm

Without a family, man, alone in the world, trembles with the cold.

—*André Malraux*

❧

I know why families were created, with all their imperfections. They humanize you. They are made to make you forget yourself occasionally, so that the beautiful balance of life is not destroyed.

—*Anais Nin*

❧

Home is where the heart is.

—*Pliny*

❧

To maintain a joyful family requires much from both the parents and the children. Each member of the family has to become, in a special way, the servant of the others.

—*Pope John Paul II*

66

The family that prays together, stays together.

—Proverb

The family is one of nature's masterpieces.

—George Santayana

Family life! The United Nations is child's play compared to the tugs and splits and the need to understand and forgive in any family.

—Mary Sarton

Large family; quick help.

—Serbian Proverb

Like all cultures, one of the family's
first jobs is to persuade its members
they're special, more wonderful
than the neighboring barbarians. The
persuasion consists of stories showing
family members demonstrating
admirable traits, which it claims are
family traits. Attention to the stories'
actual truth is never the family's most
compelling consideration. Encouraging
belief is. The family's survival depends
on the shared sensibility of its members.

−Elizabeth Stone

8

CHILD GUIDANCE

Perhaps I may record here my protest against the efforts, so often made, to shield children and young people from all that has to do with death and sorrow, to give them a good time at all hazards on the assumption that the ills of life will come soon enough. Young people themselves often resent this attitude on the part of their elders; they feel set aside and belittled as if they were denied common human experiences.

—*Jane Addams*

Education commences at the mother's knee and every word spoken in the hearing of little children tends toward the formation of character. Let parents always bear this in mind.

—*H. Ballou*

There is a widespread refusal to let children know that the source of much that goes wrong with life is due to our very own natures—the propensity of all men for acting aggressively, asocially, selfishly, out of anger and anxiety. Instead, we want our children to believe that inherently all men are good; and often, even when they are, they would prefer not to be. This contradicts what they are told by their parents, and therefore makes the child a monster in his own eyes.

—*Bruno Bettelheim*

Most mothers think that to keep young people away from lovemaking it is enough never to speak of it in their presence.

—*Marie Madeleine de Lafayette*

If it is desirable that children be kind, appreciative, and pleasant, then those qualities should be taught—not hoped for.

—*James Dobson*

∽∾

Children miss nothing in sizing up their parents. If you are only half convinced of your beliefs, they will quickly discern that fact.

—*James Dobson*

∽∾

It is the responsibility of every adult . . . to make sure that children hear what we have learned from the lessons of life.

—*Marian Wright Edelman*

∽∾

If you would persuade, you must appeal to interest rather than intellect.

—*Ben Franklin*

T he best time to give swimming
lessons is not when someone
is drowning.

—*Dr. Haim Ginott*

❧

I f adults are not comfortable enough
to talk about sex and contraceptives
with their children, they should learn.
Otherwise they might have babies
running around the house.

—*Girl, age 16*

❧

N o one has yet fully realized the
wealth of sympathy, kindness, and
generosity hidden in the soul of a
child. The effort of every true
education should be to unlock
that treasure.

—*Emma Goldman*

The adult world is . . . built on the shifting grounds of friendship and competition. The double message of the society and economy is to get along and get ahead. We want our children to fit in and stand out. We rarely address the conflict between these goals.

—*Ellen Goodman*

The best kind of sex education is life in a loving family.

—*Rosemary Haughton*

I must say that the biggest lesson you can learn in life, or teach your children, is that life is not castles in the skies, happily ever after. The biggest lesson we have to give our children is truth. And that's what I'm saying: that we've all built with illusions. And they break.

—*Goldie Hawn*

Parents think their children should keep their innocence as long as possible. The world doesn't work that way. If parents ever have a choice between mentioning something to children or not mentioning something to children, they should mention it. That's a choice between talking and not talking; always choose talking, even if it is more difficult.

—Grace Hechinger

The highest result of education is tolerance.

—Helen Keller

Character cannot be developed in ease and quiet. Only through experience of trial and suffering can the soul be strengthened, vision cleared, ambition inspired, and success achieved.

—Helen Keller

76

Civilization is just a slow process of learning to be kind.

—*Charles L. Lucas*

Good character is more to be praised than outstanding talent. Most talents are, to some extent, a gift. Good character, by contrast, is not given to us. We have to build it piece by piece—by thought, choice, courage, and determination.

—*John Luther*

The best sex education for kids is when Daddy pats Mommy on the fanny when he comes home from work.

—*Dr. William H. Masters*

The purpose of all civilization is to convert man, a beast of prey, into a tame and civilized animal.

—*Friedrich Nietzsche*

Train up a child in the way he should go, and when he is old he will not depart from it.

—*Proverbs 22:6*

When it comes to children using harmful substances, a parent's two biggest enemies are ignorance and denial.

—*Dr. Timothy Rivinus*

You gain strength, courage, and confidence by every experience in which you really stop to look fear in the face. You are able to say to yourself, "I have lived through this horror. I can take the next thing that comes along." You must do the thing you think you cannot do.

—Eleanor Roosevelt

Do but gain a boy's trust; convince him by your behavior that you have his happiness at heart; let him discover that you are the wiser of the two; let him experience the benefits of following your advice and the evils that arise from disregarding it; and fear not you will readily enough guide him.

—Herbert Spencer

In automobile terms, the child
supplies the power but the
parents have to do the steering.

—*Dr. Benjamin Spock*

※

Children require guidance and
sympathy far more than instruction.

—*Annie Sullivan*

※

It is a great mistake, I think, to put
children off with falsehoods and
nonsense, when their growing
powers of observation and
discrimination excite in them a
desire to know about things.

—*Annie Sullivan*

Healthy children are, among other things, little animals, who only slowly evolve (if they ever do) into civilized human beings. . . . Children are not naturally "good" according to any standards ever set by a civilized society. They are natural barbarians.

—*Dorothy Thompson*

I have found the best way to give advice to your children is to find out what they want and then advise them to do it.

—*Harry S. Truman*

Tell your kids again and again not to even think about trying cocaine or crack, even once.

—*Zig Ziglar*

9

PARENT/CHILD
COMMUNICATION

Listening to your children is like shopping in the bargain basement; you get a lot of things you didn't know you needed—and at a very good price.

—*Anonymous*

∽∾

If you don't understand my silence, you'll never understand what I say.

—*Anonymous*

∽∾

Society would be a delightful thing if only people were interested in each other.

—*S. R. N. Chamfort*

∽∾

We never talked, my family. We communicated by putting Ann Landers articles on the refrigerator.

—*Judy Gold*

Level with your child by being honest. Nobody spots a phony quicker than a child.

—*Mary MacCracken*

∞

The greatest cruelty that can be inflicted on children is to refuse to let them express their anger and suffering except at the risk of losing their parent's love and affection.

—*Alice Miller*

∞

Listening is not merely not talking, though even that is beyond most of our powers; it means taking a vigorous, human interest in what is being told us. You can listen like a blank wall or like a splendid auditorium where every sound comes back fuller and richer.

—*Alice Duer Miller*

86

P erhaps the most critical sexual
abuse prevention strategy for
parents is good communication
with your children.
*—National Center on
Child Abuse and Neglect*

C hildren can't be expected to leave
the unhappy and angry parts of
themselves at the door before coming
in. We all need to feel that we can
bring the whole of ourselves to the
people who care about us.
—Fred Rogers

I t is not enough for parents to understand children. They must accord
children the privilege of understanding them.
—Milton R. Sapirstein

T he first duty of love is to listen.
—Paul Tillich

10

PARENT/CHILD RELATIONSHIP

The best inheritance a parent can give his children is a few minutes of his time each day.

—*O. A. Battista*

We come into this world alone, and alone we leave it; and between the entrance and the exit, we spend our time looking for companionship.

—*E. M. Dooling*

The secret of parentage is the ability to be young again, to throw off all dignity and degree and to play on an honest equality with the child.

—*Will Durant*

If you don't eat at least one meal with your children, you give up your best opportunity to teach concern for the needs of theirs. Let's face it, chaotic meals contribute to self-oriented, pleasure-oriented values. The family meal is an excellent forum to learn about listening to others, taking turns, and in general constraining instinctual needs in a social context.

—Dr. Lawrence J. Hatterer

My advice to moms is to plan one special day for your child and do whatever the child wants for fun. Only take one child at a time and don't do any errands, do something fun and special.

—Holly, age 12

Your children need your presence
more than they need your presents.
—Jesse Jackson

❧

Learning how to behave—and to be
more comfortable behaving that
way—depends on parental influence
rather than power, on the warmth
and the relationship adults offer
rather than on the clarity of the
orders they impose.
—Penelope Leach

❧

When you are dealing with a child,
keep your wits about you, and sit on
the floor.
—Austin O'Malley

Romance fails us and so do friendships, but the relationship of parent and child, less noisy than all others, remains indelible and indestructible, the strongest relationship on earth.

—*Theodor Reik*

❧

I wish I would have put as much emotion into my relationships with my mom and dad as I do now into my memories of them. We should pay more attention when we are making our memories. If we did, we wouldn't have so many regrets when all we have are memories.

—*Sixty-year-old Woman*

94

Fellow citizens, why do you turn
and scrape every stone to gather
wealth and take so little care of your
children, to whom one day you must
relinquish it all?

—*Socrates*

It is given to man to have children,
but to comparatively few to know
and understand them and to be com-
panions to them.

—*D. A. Thom*

We are always too busy for our
children; we never give them the
time or interest they deserve. We
lavish gifts upon them, but the
most precious gift—our personal
association, which means so much
to them—we give grudgingly.

—*Mark Twain*

11

PARENTAL MATURITY

If you command yourself, you command the world.

—Chinese Proverb

❧

The value of marriage is not that adults produce children but that children produce adults.

—Peter de Vries

❧

No one is free who commands not himself.

—Epictetus

❧

Healthy children will not fear life if their elders have integrity enough to fear death.

—Erik Erikson

You can learn many things from children. How much patience you have, for instance.

— *Frank P. Jones*

❦

Parents who expect gratitude from their children (there are even some who insist on it) are like insurers who gladly risk their capital if only they receive interest.

— *Franz Kafka*

❦

I looked on child rearing not only as a work of love and duty but as a profession that was fully as interesting and challenging as any honorable profession in the world and one that demanded the best that I could bring to it.

— *Rose Kennedy*

The real menace in dealing
with a five-year-old is that in no
time at all you begin to sound like
a five-year-old.

—*Jean Kerr*

To be a good parent, you have to
put yourself second, to recognize
that the child has feelings and
needs separate from yours, and
fulfill those needs without expecting
anything in return.

—*Howard Kogan*

Remember, when they have a
tantrum, don't have one of your own.

—*Dr. Judith Kuriansky*

When we can begin to take our failures non-seriously, it means we are ceasing to be afraid of them. It is of immense importance to learn to laugh at ourselves.

—Katherine Mansfield

God knows that a mother needs fortitude and courage and tolerance and flexibility and patience and firmness and nearly every other brave aspect of the human soul. But because I happen to be a parent of an almost fiercely maternal nature, I praise casualness. It seems to me the rarest of virtues. It is useful enough when children are small. It is important to the point of necessity when they are adolescents.

—Phyllis McGinley

Most of us become parents
long before we have stopped
being children.

—*Mignon McLoughlin*

It is difficult to give children a
sense of security unless you have
it yourself. If you have it, they
catch it from you.

—*Dr. William C. Menninger*

One face to the world, another
at home makes for misery.

—*Amy Vanderbilt*

12

PARENTS AS TEACHERS

One of the greatest disappointments in raising my children is that we lived in the suburbs, a homogenized strip of cornfield where everyone was the same color, the same religion, drove the same station wagon with the wood on it, voted the same ticket, and made monthly payments on the same style of cookie-cutter house.

—*Erma Bombeck*

A scholar is of all persons the most unfit to teach young children. A mother is the infant's true guide to knowledge.

—*Edward Bulwer-Lytton*

The most important thing is to teach your child compassion. A complete human being is one who can put himself in another's shoes.

—*Bessie and Sadie Delany,*
ages 101 and 103

Parents have become so convinced that educators know what is best for children that they forget that they themselves are really the experts.

—*Marian Wright Edelman*

Be careful to leave your sons well instructed rather then rich, for the hopes of the instructed are better than the wealth of the ignorant.

—*Epictetus*

Education begins at home. You can't blame the school for not putting into your child what you don't put into him. You don't just take your child to ballet class. First, you dance with him, when he's a baby. Every family has its own rhythm, and if you dance with your children, that rhythm will become a part of them, and they will never forget it.

—*Geoffrey Holder*

Man's mind once stretched by
a new idea never regains its
original dimension.

—Oliver Wendell Holmes

I am part of all I have read.

—John Kieran

The important thing is not so much
that every child should be taught, as
that every child should be given the
wish to learn.

—John Lubbock

Education alone can conduct us to
that enjoyment which is, at once, best
in quality and infinite in quantity.

—Horace Mann

You are the same today that you'll
be five years from now except for
two things: the people you meet and
the books you read.

—*Mae McMillan*

ⓢ⁄ⓢ

There are many little ways to
enlarge [your child's] world. Love
of books is the best of all.

—*Jacqueline Kennedy Onassis*

ⓢ⁄ⓢ

Don't limit your child to your
own learning, for he was born in
another time.

—*Rabbinical Saying*

Helping your eldest to pick a college is one of the greatest educational experiences of life—for the parents. Next to trying to pick his bride, it's the best way to learn that your authority, if not entirely gone, is slipping fast.

—*Sally and James Reston*

Do not reason coldly with youth. Clothe your reason with a body if you would make it felt. Let the mind speak the language of the heart, that it may be understood.

—*Jean-Jacques Rousseau*

A child educated only at school is an uneducated child.

—*George Santayana*

We speak of educating our children. Do we know that our children also educate us?

—*Mrs. Sigourney*

111

13

PARENTAL
RIGHTS/NEEDS

The thing I liked least about my mother was that she was always giving the most.

—*Anonymous*

❧

Don't demand respect, as a parent. Demand civility and insist on honesty. But respect is something you must earn—with kids as well as with adults.

—*William Attwood*

❧

Love yourself first and everything else falls into line. You really have to love yourself to get anything done in this world.

—*Lucille Ball*

Adequate parents must be adequate partners, and before a person can be an adequate partner, he must be an adequate person.

—Henry Brandt

❧

I do not believe in a child's world. . . . I believe the child should be taught from the very first that the whole world is his world, that adult and child share one world, that all generations are needed.

—Pearl S. Buck

❧

I love people. I love my family, my children . . . but inside myself is a place where I live all alone and that's where you renew your springs that never dry up.

—Pearl S. Buck

You have the right to make mistakes bringing up your own children. Blunder bravely! Go ahead and make your mistakes, but believe more bravely that, on the whole, you are doing a good job of raising your children.

You have a right to pursue your own career and interests. If you don't meet your own needs, you are not going to meet your [children's].

You have a right to be yourself. Allow your child to be himself, and you will raise a happy and psychologically healthy individual. The same reasoning applies to you as a parent. So raise your child in your own unique way. Have the courage to be yourself—as a husband or a wife, above all, as a parent.

—*Fitzhugh Dodson*

The thing that most people don't understand about child rearing is that what you do deliberately as a parent doesn't matter as much as who you are, and kids have a way of finding that out.

—*Richard Farson*

The way for us to help our children is to help ourselves. The way for us to respect our children is to respect ourselves.

—*Lorraine Hale*
(daughter of Mother Clara Hale)

Parents cannot effectively give children what they do not have to give. When parents are too stressed, or too unfulfilled, or too guilty to take their own needs into account, the children suffer.

—*Dr. Marilyn Heins and*
Dr. Anne Marie Seiden

118

Nothing has a stronger influence
psychologically on their environment,
and especially on their children, than
the unlived life of the parents.

—*Carl Jung*

Never allow your child to call you
by your first name. He hasn't known
you long enough.

—*Fran Lebowitz*

But children can't be a center of life
and a reason for being. They can be
a thousand things that are delightful,
interesting, satisfying, but they can't
be a wellspring to live from. Or they
shouldn't be.

—*Doris Lessing*

When your schedule leaves you brain-drained and stressed to exhaustion, it's time to give up something! Delegate. Say no. Be brutal. It's like cleaning out a closet—after a while it gets easier to get rid of things. You discover that you really didn't need them anyway.

—*Marilyn Ruman*

The best upbringing that children can receive is to observe their parents taking excellent care of themselves—mind, body, spirit. Children, being the world's greatest mimics, naturally and automatically model their parents' behavior.

—*Dr. Benjamin Spock*

You have to take the time to be a whole person if you want to rear your children to be whole.

—*Della White Steele*

The good-enough mother is one who takes care of herself so that she has something to give.

—*Marie Wilson*

14

PROMOTING
CHILD AUTONOMY

You can let go of your children
only when there are no conditions
attached to your love for them and
when you truly accept that their
rights and responsibilities are the
same as your own.

—*Jane Addams*

If you want something very, very
badly, let it go free. If it comes back
to you, it's yours forever. If it doesn't,
it was never yours to begin with.

—*Anonymous*

Nothing grows well in the shade
of a big tree.

—*Constantin Brancusi*

There are only two lasting bequests
we can hope to give our children.
One of these is roots. The other wings.
                              —Hodding Carter

❧

The mother-women seemed to
prevail that summer at Grand Isle.
It was easy to know them, fluttering
about with extended, protecting wings
when any harm, real or imaginary,
threatened their precious brood. They
were women who idolized their
children, worshiped their husbands,
and esteemed it a holy privilege to
efface themselves as individuals and
grow wings as ministering angels.
                              —Kate Chopin
                    The Awakening, *1889*

The most important thing that parents can teach their children is how to get along without them.

—*Frank A. Clark*

ⓢ⁄ⓢ

Children have to be educated, but they have also to be left to educate themselves.

—*Abbé Dimnet*

ⓢ⁄ⓢ

The greatest gift you can give your child is the freedom to actualize his unique potential self.

—*Fitzhugh Dodson*

ⓢ⁄ⓢ

If you want to see what children can do, you must stop giving them things.

—*Norman Douglas*

127

The sooner you treat your son as a man, the sooner he will be one.

—*John Dryden*

＊

The finest inheritance you can give to a child is to allow it to make its own way, completely on its own feet.

—*Isadora Duncan*

＊

A mother is not a person to lean on but a person to make leaning unnecessary.

—*Dorothy Canfield Fisher*

＊

Let your children go if you want to keep them.

—*Malcolm Forbes*

The mother-child relationship is paradoxical and, in a sense, tragic. It requires the most intense love on the mother's side, yet this very love must help the child to grow away from the mother and to become fully independent.

—*Erich Fromm*

Your children are not your children. They are the sons and daughters of Life's longing for itself.

—*Kahlil Gibran*

Let there be spaces in your togetherness.

—*Kahlil Gibran*

You may give them your love but not your thoughts, for they have their own thoughts. You may house their bodies but not their souls, for their souls dwell in the house of tomorrow which you cannot visit, not even in your dreams. You may strive to be like them, but seek not to make them like you. For life goes not backward nor tarries with yesterday. You are the bows from which your children as living arrows are sent forth.

—Kahlil Gibran

Children occasionally need the sort of benevolent neglect that allows a flower to choose its own time and place to blossom.

—Sally James

130

If you love your son, make him leave home.

—*Japanese Proverb*

At every step the child should be allowed to meet the real experiences of life; the thorns should never be plucked from his roses.

—*Ellen Key*

It is not what you do for your children but what you have taught them to do for themselves that will make them successful human beings.

—*Ann Landers*

We have kept our children so busy with "useful" and "improving" activities that we are in danger of raising a generation of young people who are terrified of silence, of being alone with their own thoughts.

—Eda LeShan

Never help a child with a task at which he feels he can succeed.

—Maria Montessori

"Letting our children go" is a life-long process for parents, one that we wrestle with again and again, and each parent has to wrestle with it in his or her own way.

—Fred Rogers

One of the most important gifts a parent can give a child is the gift of that child's uniqueness.

—Fred Rogers

❧

Love him (or her) and let her (or him) alone. Let him enjoy his troubled moments. He may need an occasional withdrawal or self-inquiry. Don't intrude upon the private mood. It does not necessarily mean he hates you or resents his mother or should be carried off to a couch.

—Leo C. Rosten

❧

Be aware that young people have to be able to make their own mistakes and that times change.

—Gina Shapira

You are a parent only when you provide for and prepare your child to be ready for life.

—*Joy Strack*

☙❧

The more you love your children, the more care you should take to neglect them occasionally. The web of affection can be drawn too tight.

—*D. Sutten*

☙❧

If you want a baby, have a new one. Don't baby the old one.

—*Jessamyn West*

15

REALISTIC
PARENTAL
EXPECTATIONS

A child is like a precious stone, but also a heavy burden.

—*African (Swahili) Proverb*

One doesn't rise to low expectations.

—*Anonymous*

We are not trying to educate children and send them into the world as finished products—we send them forward as a person well begun.

—*Sr. Angela Boyo*

Aim for success, not perfection. Never give up your right to be wrong, because then you will lose the ability to learn new things and move forward with your life. Remember that fear always lurks behind perfectionism.

—*Dr. David Burns*

While everything else in our lives has gotten simpler, speedier, more microwavable and user-friendly, child raising seems to have expanded to fill the time no longer available for it.

—*Barbara Ehrenreich*

An atmosphere of trust, love, and humor can nourish extraordinary human capacity. One key is authenticity: parents acting as people, not as roles.

—*Marilyn Ferguson*

Parents can only give good advice or put them on the right paths, but the final forming of a person's character lies in their own hands.

—*Anne Frank*

Insecure is my new role, I was at
odds with—and battered by—an ideal
of the breezy, capable mother I
assumed everyone else was. I could
handle myself at important meetings,
meet tough deadlines, argue fluently
in French. Why couldn't I keep
Cheerios off the kitchen floor?

—Leslie George

Living with a saint is more grueling
than being one.

—Robert Neville

The essence of being human is that
one does not seek perfection.

—George Orwell

Our children give us the opportunity to become the parent we always wish we had.

—A Parent

❧

The good thing about parenthood is that, one way or another, you always get another chance to show what you learned.

—Nancy Samalin

❧

One hour with a child is like a ten-mile run.

—Joan Benoit Samuelson

❧

The damnable frustration of raising kids is that you never can tell if you are doing things right.

—J. D. Sanderson

The ideal mother, like the ideal marriage, is fiction.

—*Milton R. Sapirstein*

☙❧

Don't try so hard! I think that many mothers try to be the perfect stereotype mother. They're always doing things that they think will make their children happy. Some mothers get so involved that their whole world revolves around their kids. I say, go out and have some fun. Go dancing, you can afford to hire a babysitter on occasion. Just because you have children doesn't mean that your whole life has to end.

—*Sarah, age 13*

Babies don't come with directions on the back or batteries that can be removed. Motherhood is twenty-four hours a day, seven days a week. You can't "leave the office."

—*Pat Schroeder*

The best brought-up children are those who have seen their parents as they are.

—*George Bernard Shaw*

Do not try to produce an ideal child; it would find no fitness in this world.

—*Herbert Spencer*

Y ou know more than you think
you do.

−Dr. Benjamin Spock

S o don't worry about trying to do
a perfect job. There is no perfect job.
There is no one way of raising
your children.

−Dr. Benjamin Spock

A baby is an inestimable blessing
and bother.

−Mark Twain

L ittle children disturb your sleep,
big ones, your life.

−Yiddish Proverb

RESPECTING
YOUR CHILD

Parenting forms children's core belief about themselves. Nothing could be more important.

—*John Bradshaw*

❧

But it is really true that you can get by without much money. We had love and respect and all those good things.

—*Sadie Delany*

❧

The willingness to accept responsibility for one's own life is the source from which self-respect springs.

—*Joan Didion*

❧

Thou shalt not belittle your child.

—*Fitzhugh Dodson*

When we are polite to children, we show in the most simple and direct way possible that we value them as people and care about their feelings.

—*David Elkind*

Respect the child. Be not too much his parent. Trespass not on his solitude.

—*R. W. Emerson*

The potential of every child is unimaginable, yet by trying to imagine it, we can help that child reach toward it.

—*Linda and Richard Eyre*

The whole life of the individual is nothing but the process of giving birth to himself; indeed, we should be fully born when we die—although it is the tragic fate of most individuals to die before they are born.

—Erich Fromm

Treat children as if they were what they ought to be and you help them become what they are capable of being.

—Goethe

As for boys and girls, it is one of the sorriest mistakes to talk down to them: almost always your lad of fifteen thinks more simply, more fundamentally than you do; and what he accepts as good coin are not facts or precepts, but feelings and convictions.

—David Grayson

The parents' responsibility is not to mold, shape, pattern, or condition him, but to support him in such a way that his precious hidden uniqueness shall be able to emerge and guide his whole development.

—*Harry Guntrip*

❧

Feel the dignity of a child. Do not feel superior to him, for you are not.

—*Robert Henri*

❧

My father taught me that you never talk down to your audience. So I've always talked to kids like they were adults.

—*Peter Jennings*

Children are likely to live up to what you believe of them.

—*Lady Bird Johnson*

❧

In some families, *please* is described as the magic word. In our house, however, it was *sorry*.

—*Margaret Lawrence*

❧

Too many parents emphasize what babies can do rather than glorying in the people they are becoming.

—*Penelope Leach*

❧

He that will have his son have respect for him and his orders, must himself have a great reverence for his son.

—*John Locke*

The most important aspect of living with a child is the respect you convey for that child as an individual.

—*Millicent McIntosh*

❧

Every child has a need to be noticed, understood, taken seriously, and respected.

—*Alice Miller*

❧

We all grew up in a pedagogical system in which the child's narcissistic needs for respect, mirroring, understanding, and self-expression were neither recognized nor tolerated; on the contrary, they were stifled. Nevertheless, we can still attempt to gain a new outlook.

—*Alice Miller*

All children wear the sign: "I want
to be important NOW." Many of our
juvenile delinquency problems arise
because nobody reads the sign.

—*Dan Pursuit*

∞

If the day ever came when we were
able to accept ourselves and our children exactly as we and they
are, then I believe we would have
come very close to an ultimate
understanding of what "good"
parenting means.

—*Fred Rogers*

∞

We worry about what a child will
be tomorrow, yet we forget that he
is someone today.

—*Stacia Tauscher*

It is a shameful thing to insult a little child. It has its feelings, it has its small dignity; and since it cannot defend them, it is surely an ignoble act to injure them.

—*Mark Twain*

RESPONSIBILITY
IN CHILDREN

No one would have crossed the ocean if he could have gotten off the ship in the storm.

—*Anonymous*

It isn't easy to be the person who sometimes has to try to preserve your happiness at the expense of your fun.

—*Margaret Culkin Banning*

It is poor encouragement to toil through life to amass a fortune to ruin your children. In nine cases out of ten, a large fortune is the greatest curse which could be bequeathed to the young and inexperienced.

—*Bruyere*

157

A gem is not polished without friction, nor man perfected without trials.
—Chinese Proverb

Children learn to be responsible by seeing their parents do things that are difficult or hard to do.
—Harris Clemes, Ph.D., and
Reynold Bean, Ed.M.

All of us children had chores to do, and Papa always saw to it that we did them.
—Sadie Delany

Where parents do too much for their children, the children will not do much for themselves.
—Elbert Hubbard

Whenever we are doing for the
child what the child can easily do
for himself, we are in the way of his
development.

—*Maria Montessori*

❧

A mother who spoils her child
fattens a serpent.

—*Spanish Proverb*

❧

A spoilt child never loves
his mother.

—*Henry Taylor*

SELF-DISCIPLINED
CHILDREN

The poorest education that teaches
self-control is better than the best that
neglects it.

—*Anonymous*

❦

Conquer thyself. Till thou has done
this, thou art but a slave; for it is
almost as well to be subjected to
another's appetite as to thine own.

—*Sir Richard Francis Burton*

❦

What is the best government? That
which teaches us to govern ourselves.

—*Goethe*

163

The secret of all success is to know how to deny yourself. Prove that you can control yourself, and you are an educated man, and without this all other education is good for nothing.

—R. D. Hitchcock

❧

Perhaps the most valuable result of all education is the ability to make yourself do the things you have to do, when they ought to be done, whether you like it or not; it is the first lesson that ought to be learned; and however early a man's training begins, it is probably the last lesson he learns thoroughly.

—Thomas Henry Huxley

❧

Teach your child to deny himself.

—Gen. Robert E. Lee

No child is born with self-discipline.
                                    —*Fred Rogers*

Do all in your power to teach your
children self-government.
                                    —*William B. Sprague*

Make it a point to do something
every day that you don't want
to do. This is the golden rule
for acquiring the habit of doing
your duty without pain.
                                    —*Mark Twain*

19

SPARKING YOUR CHILD'S INTERESTS

We're constantly striving for success, fame, and comfort when all we really need to be happy is someone or something to be enthusiastic about.

—*Anonymous*

Years may wrinkle the skin. Lack of enthusiasm will wrinkle the soul.

—*Anonymous*

A group of two hundred executives was asked what makes a person successful: eighty percent listed enthusiasm as the most important quality.

—*Anonymous*

If you can give your son or daughter only one gift, let it be enthusiasm.

—*Bruce Barton*

If a child is to keep alive his inborn sense of wonder, he needs the companionship of at least one adult who can share it, rediscovering with him the joy, excitement, and mystery of the world we live in.

—Rachel Carson

Choose a job you love, and you will never have to work a day in your life.

—Confucius

Only passions, great passions, can elevate the soul to great things.

—Denis Diderot

I told the kids in Taos High School that day to trust in what they loved, that you don't know where it will lead you. The important thing is to love something, even if it's skateboarding or car mechanics or whistling. Let yourself love it completely.

—*Natalie Goldberg*

Nothing is work unless you'd rather be doing something else.

—*George Halas*

Allow children to be happy their own way: for what better way will they ever find?

—*Samuel Johnson*

To be successful, the first thing to do is fall in love with your work.

—*Sister Mary Lauretta*

Follow your own bent, no matter what people say.

—*Karl Marx*

❧

Neither a lofty degree of intelligence nor imagination nor both together go to the making of genius. Love, love, love, that is the soul of genius.

—*Wolfgang Amadeus Mozart*

❧

Do not train boys to learning by force and harshness, but lead them by what amuses them, so that they may better discover the best of their minds.

—*Plato*

❧

Don't ever let me catch you singing like that again, without enthusiasm. You're nothing if you aren't excited by what you're doing.

—*Frank Sinatra,
to his son, Frank, Jr.*

HUMAN VALUES

Always be a little kinder than necessary.

—*James M. Barrie*

Recommend to your children *virtue*; that alone can make them happy, not gold.

—*Ludwig von Beethoven*

We are born with only the *potential* to be human.

—*Robert Carkhuff*

Every boy, in his heart, would rather steal second base than an automobile.

—*Judge Tom Clark*

What you do not want done to
yourself, do not do to others.
—*Confucius*

All of the values that made us
strong came from the church. It was
religious faith that formed the back-
bone of the Delany family.
—*Bessie and Sadie Delany*

It's not hard to make decisions when
you know what your values are.
—*Roy Disney*

I believe the most valuable
contribution a parent can make
to his child is to instill in him a
genuine faith in God. What greater
ego satisfaction could there be than
knowing that the creator of the
universe is acquainted with
me personally?

—*James Dobson*

People should think less about
what they ought to do and more
about what they ought to be. If only
their living were good, their work
would shine forth brightly.

—*Meister Eckhart*

Our children are growing up now
in an ethically polluted nation where
substance is being sacrificed daily for
shadow.

—*Marian Wright Edelman*

Teach your children good manners. *Please* and *thank you* are two of the most important words in the English language. Being considerate of others will take you and them further in life than any college or professional degree.

—*Marian Wright Edelman*

❦

Be moral examples for your children. If you as parents cut corners, your children will too. If you lie, they will too.

—*Marian Wright Edelman*

❦

We should teach values to our children because it is the most significant and effective thing we can do for their happiness.

—*Linda and Richard Eyre*

178

The home will never, should never, can never be replaced as the institution where basic values are learned and taught.

—*Linda and Richard Eyre*

Those who stand for nothing fall for anything.

—*Alexander Hamilton*

I know only that what is moral is what you feel good after and what is immoral is what you feel bad after.

—*Ernest Hemingway*

In matters of style, swim with the current; in matters of principle, stand like a rock.

—*Thomas Jefferson*

All things whatsoever ye would that men should do to you, do ye even so to them: for this is the Law and the Prophets.

—*Jesus of Nazareth*

Many persons have a wrong idea of what constitutes true happiness. It is not attained through self-gratification but through fidelity to a worthy purpose.

—*Helen Keller*

Man must evolve for all human conflict a method which rejects revenge, aggression, and retaliation. The foundation of such a method is love.

—*Martin Luther King, Jr.*

The loveliest fairy in the world;
and her name is Mrs.
Doasyouwouldbedoneby.

—*Charles Kingsley*

❧

As parents explain, again and
again, the few and vitally important
values that underpin their everyday
exhortations about trivia, children
measure their words against their
actions and take the values that they
see truly held unto themselves.

—*Penelope Leach*

❧

It has become more important to
be a smart kid than a good kid
or even a healthy kid.

—*Sam Levenson*

When we are planning for posterity, we ought to remember that virtue is not hereditary.

—*Thomas Paine*

❧

Begin to instruct as soon as a child has any notion of the difference between good and evil. And this is as soon as he knows your smile from your frown.

—*Samuel Palmer*

❧

Education in virtue is the only education which deserves the name.

—*Plato*

❧

Educate the heart—educate the heart. Let us have good men.

—*Hiram Powers*

182

If parents want honest children, they should be honest themselves.

—Proverb

❧

The truly important ingredients of life are still the same as they always have been—true love and real friendship, honesty and faithfulness, sincerity, unselfishness and selflessness, the concept that it is better to give than to receive, to do unto others as you would have them do unto you. These principles are still around; they haven't gone away.

—Nancy Reagan

❧

The conscience of children is formed by the influences that surround them; their notions of good and evil are the result of the moral atmosphere they breathe.

—Conrad Richter

Peace is not an absence of war, it is a virtue, a state of mind, a disposition for benevolence, confidence, justice.

—*Benedict Spinoza*

They who give the world a true philosophy, a grand poem, a beautiful painting or statue, or can tell the story of every wandering star . . . have lived to a holier purpose than they whose children have breathed no clear perception of great principles, no moral aspiration, no spiritual life.

—*Elizabeth Cady Stanton*

The parents who transmit altruism most effectively . . . exert a firm control over their children. Although they are nurturant, they are not permissive. They use a combination of firmness, warmth, and reasoning. They point out to children the consequences to others of misbehavior—and good behavior, and they actively guide the child to do good, to share, to be helpful.

—Ervin Staub

❧

Teaching kids to count is fine, but teaching them what counts is best.

—Bob Talbert

❧

Be careful how you live. You may be the only Bible some person ever reads.

—William J. Toms

185

21

STRONG MARITAL RELATIONSHIP

A good husband is never first to go to sleep at night or the last to awake in the morning.

—Honoré de Balzac

Being a husband is a whole-time job.

—Arnold Bennett

The best security blanket a child can have is parents who respect each other.

—Jan Blaustane

Marriage is an empty box. It remains empty unless you put in more than you take out.

—H. Jackson Brown, Jr.

To keep the fire burning brightly there's one easy rule: keep the two logs together, near enough to keep each other warm and far enough apart—about a finger's breadth—for breathing room. Good fire, good marriage, same rule.

—Marie Reed Crowel

Spoil your husband, but don't spoil your children—that's my philosophy.

—Louise Currey,
on being chosen Mother of the Year, 1961.

Of course I don't always enjoy being a mother. At those times my husband and I hole up somewhere in the wine country, eat, drink, make mad love, and pretend we were born sterile and raise poodles.

—Dorothy DeBolt,
on receiving the National Mother's Day Committee Award as the natural mother of 6 and adoptive mother of 14, 1980

190

A sound marriage is not based on complete frankness; it is based on sensible reticence.

—Morris L. Ernst

Husbands are like fires. They go out when unattended.

—Zsa Zsa Gabor

Better the child should cry than the father.

—German Proverb

The most important thing a father can do for his children is to love their mother.

—Rev. Theodore Hesburgh

191

All married couples should learn
the art of battle as they should learn
the art of making love. Good battle
is objective and honest—never vicious
or cruel. Good battle is healthy and
constructive, and brings to a marriage
the principle of equal partnership.

—*Ann Landers*

However rare true love may be, it
is less so than true friendship.

—*François La Rochefoucauld*

A successful marriage is an edifice
that must be rebuilt every day.

—*André Maurois*

Moms, start liking those ex-
husbands of yours. It would make
your kids happier.

—*Megan, age 11*

Y ou have to work constantly at
rejuvenating a relationship. You can't
just count on its being o.k.; or it will
tend toward a hollow commitment,
devoid of passion and intimacy.
People need to put the kind of ener-
gy into it that they put into their children or career.

—*Dr. Robert Sternberg*

N early all marriages, even happy
ones, are mistakes: in the sense that
almost certainly (in a more perfect
world, or even with a little more
care in this very imperfect one)
both partners might have found
more suitable mates. But the real
soulmate is the one you are
actually married to.

—*J. R. R. Tolkien*

RAISING SIBLINGS

Comparison is a death knell to
sibling harmony.

—Elizabeth Fiskel

If you have a pet child, send
him traveling.

—Japanese Proverb

Never praise a sister to a sister,
in the hope of your compliments
reaching the proper ears.

—Rudyard Kipling

He who singles out one child and
gives him even one more date than
he gives his other children, God shall
single him out by giving him a piece
of glowing coal.

—Lebanese Proverb

Although children say they want total equality, it's impossible to achieve, it is a hardship on parents (did you ever try counting the number of sprinkles on two ice cream cones, or the number of cheerios in two bowls of cereal?), and it is not what the children really want anyway. . . . Research has shown that a policy of providing two sisters two of everything—two swings, two sandboxes, two tricycles, two pairs of similar galoshes—does not prevent rivalry. The reason is that children are not really fighting over swings, or the cookies, or the Jordache jeans. What they are fighting over is your love. What they need is the reassurance that they have it.

—*Joan Weiss*

Index of Authors

202

About the Editor

Dr. Charles Schaefer is a nationally renowned child psychologist who is the director of a university-based mental health center in New Jersey. He is the author or coauthor of over 35 books on parenting and child psychology, including *Teach Your Child to Behave* and *How to Help Children with Common Problems.* Dr. Schaefer lives in New York with his wife Anne, and children Karine and Eric.